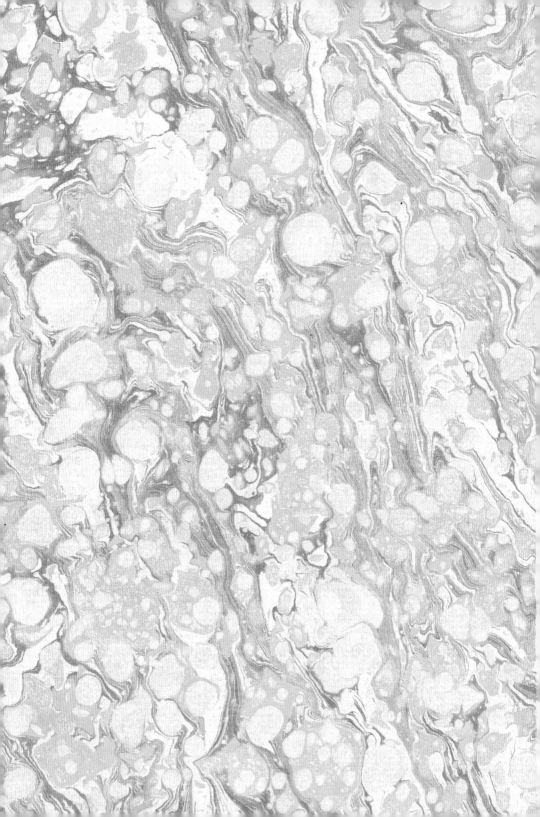

RUSKIN'S ROSE

RUSKIN'S ROSE

A VENETIAN LOVE STORY

A true tale by **MIMMA BALIA**

with **MICHELLE LOVRIC**

Collages by **ANN FIELD**

ARTISAN · NEW YORK

Published by ARTISAN
A Division of Workman Publishing Company, Inc.
708 Broadway, New York, New York 10003
www.workman.com

Library of Congress Cataloging-in-Publication Data

Lovric, Michelle.
Ruskin's rose : a Venetian love story /
Michelle Lovric.
p. cm
ISBN 1-57965-137-2
1. Ruskin, John, 1819–1900—Homes and
haunts—Italy—Venice. 2. Authors, English.
3. Venice (Italy). 4. Christmas. I. Title.
PS3562.O8765 R87 2000
813'.54—dc21   00-35530

Printed in Hong Kong
10 9 8 7 6 5 4 3 2 1

Book design by VERTIGO DESIGN, NYC

CONTENTS

INTRODUCTION

L et me take you back to Venice. The
Venice of five centuries ago, of one
century ago. The Venice of a hundred serpen-
tine canals, arching bridges, and throbbing
church bells, of artists and poets, ghosts and
reflections. . . .

Though it is called La Serenissima, Venice
is truly the least serene and most perturbing

of cities. Pass through her at your peril on your way in or out of love. Whether you are hurtling toward joy or pain, Venice will expedite your journey.

John Ruskin, the influential English art historian, in 1876 did the unsafe thing of entering Venice with a ransacked heart. At first, he found joy in writing of the floating palazzi of Venice and of her towers rising in branchless forests from the sea. But then her beautiful, strange sadness wept into his soul and he found himself "so very lonely . . . black weather and rain at last made it sadder." His friends and admirers worried about his well-being, for Ruskin was distracted by—completely lost to—the memories of his lost love in the dark streets of marble and water. It was hardly the first time Ruskin had been seduced by the city's beauty. You can, if you like, read his renowned text, *Stones of Venice,* for its art history, but it's the poetry that will ravish you.

Stones had been published twenty-five years earlier, amidst numerous other books penned by Ruskin—critical works on art, culture, and society that had made him one of Europe's prominent men of thought. His opinions were progressive for the time: He was concerned about the environment and spoke of the importance of nature to man. Of course, his notions about romance were as desperately old-fashioned as they come. The one person Ruskin deeply cared about, a young Irish girl named Rose La Touche,

 was hardly impressed by his eloquent love letters and his intelligence.

No, Rose had refused his hand in marriage, shocked by his lack of religious belief. Her refusal did not discourage his efforts in the least—nor, had it encouraged him to find God.

At the time our story begins, Ruskin had seen his first marriage scandalously annulled, lost his faith, and sat helplessly by as Rose became ill and died at age twenty-seven. He had returned to Venice to write about the spiritual side of the city as a coda to *Stones*. His greatest works were far behind him, as was the bulk of his personal fortune, given away to many philanthropic and aesthetic ventures. Still, he had fragile, intense hopes of achieving something—and forgetting about Rose. Indeed, he worked feverishly but on far too many things. He repeatedly delayed his return to England. To economize, he moved from his big rooms in the Grand Hotel to cheaper ones, and then, finally, to the humble Calcina on Zattere.

Ruskin was writing a denunciation of the bad restoration work in the Basilica of San Marco. He was making studies of the sculpted Noah at the Palazzo Ducale and of paintings in the Scuola di San Giorgio degli Schiavoni. But his diaries show that he was finding real difficulties with the major task he had set himself that year: a spiritual history of Venice. Without any spiritual belief himself, he found it a nearly impossible task.

His mood grew as dreary as the oncoming winter. Venice herself angered Ruskin: He loathed the decay, the corrupt and wrong-headed restoration. Most of all, the memory of Rose tortured him. She had wanted him pious; he merely wanted her alive.

Venice had lured him into dark rips of thought, and the water seemed to close over his eyes. He saw nothing about which he might

write—and found himself unable to put pen to paper. The voice that wove stories and filled pages was gone. *Gone away with Rosie,* he thought. Or rinsed away by tears and the slow, subtle Venetian tide. Ruskin imagined his voice, washed up on a desolate, unknown shore, runes in the sand, telling tragedies.

Then a mystical sequence of events swept away the stifling seas. He discovered a new love—hardly flesh and blood, but he'd learned his lesson about pain and didn't desire risking his heart again with this game. Through the art of a fifteenth-century painter named Vittore Carpaccio, he felt the magic touch of Rose's influence once again. Miraculously, during Christmas week of 1876, she seemed to reach out from beyond the grave. Before revealing all, however, you will need to know how Ruskin came to love—and lose—his gentle Rose.

1. Losing, Finding, Losing Love

Ruskin had known both delight and sorrow in Venice. It was the scene of a late, humiliating honeymoon in 1849, a year after he married his distant cousin Euphemia Gray. Despite the passionate letters the couple had exchanged, their union was never really tested until they said their vows and set out on a partnership that was disastrously mismatched.

Perhaps, then, it was no surprise that he didn't comment, five years later, when Effie asked that their marriage be annulled on the grounds of nonconsummation. Nor did he protest when soon thereafter she married the Pre-Raphaelite painter John Everett Millais—a man whose work Ruskin had championed.

In the face of his very public humiliation, Ruskin's career soared. He wrote with a passion, producing ever more esoteric art history for an admiring public. The pages accumulated, and he published book upon revered book.

Eventually, Ruskin fell in love again. This time he wanted a fairy tale inhabited by a fair, sweet princess. In Rose La Touche, in 1858, Ruskin had finally found the love of his life, exquisite and extreme.

Rose had first come to him in London with her mother, Maria La Touche.  Mrs. La Touche was an Irish banker's wife, a sometime novelist with pretensions to intellectual glamour and a romantic eye on the art historian. She wrote to him often as he traveled, before realizing that his interest lay not in her witty letters but in the sweetness of her ten-year-old daughter.

Before you cry out, kind reader, realize that Ruskin's love was, at first, of the most innocent kind. Still, Maria's emotions were perhaps tinged with jealousy—creating a situation that would later play out with irreversible consequences for all involved. For the time being, however, Ruskin was thirty-nine, already famous, with his marriage behind him. He needed something to believe in, and Rose was it.

She became his drawing pupil. Seventeen years of rapture and torture were about to begin. Rose was a child, yes, but precocious and already affected by a sort of religious fever. The naïveté Ruskin adored in her was already slipping away at an alarming rate. He tried to prolong her childhood with fairy tales and pet names. He called her Posie Rosie Posie. Ruskin, who liked to imagine he was a child himself, took the nickname Crumpet, later Saint Crumpet, because of his kindness to beggars. And Mrs. La Touche he named Lacerta, the supple lizard with the grace and wisdom of a snake but none of its poison. At least, not back then.

Rose shelled little pink shrimps for him at endless teatimes. They played together—or at the time, Ruskin thought he was just playing. But, over the years, he began to fall in love, an unwilling, querulous, fearful love.

By 1862, Ruskin's mania had become Rose. Rose metaphors perfumed his art criticism. A rose blossomed on the title page of his lecture notes. Rose puns invaded his letters. Nervously, he monitored Rose's adolescence. *Women have changed into flowers, why not flowers into women?* he mused.

Before he had a chance to see what would happen, Ruskin found himself without access to Rose as her parents began to think that all was not right and orthodox. A now-fourteen-year-old Rose was removed from Ruskin's presence for several desperate months. The teatimes were then permitted to begin again, only to be curtailed. Sometimes he was permitted to write to her, sometimes to see her. These sudden welcomes and incomprehensible dismissals destroyed his serenity—possibly forever—but did not alter his love for Rose.

On the occassion of Rose's eighteenth birthday, on January 4, 1866, Ruskin proposed marriage. Rose wanted three years to think about it. (Remember this number. . . .) Rose had scented incriminating wafts of atheism in his letters. Now she asked, "How could one love you—if you were a pagan?" Another time she said that she would see him if he would love God more than he loved her. Ruskin rejected this possibility. To the La Touches' eyes he was branded with a crisscross of black marks: his age, his agnosticism, the scandal of the annulled marriage, the whispers of impotence.

Though they were separated again, Ruskin held on to the hope that Rose would be his on her twenty-first birthday. He wanted her "for Wife—for Child—for Queen—for any Shape of fellow-spirit that her soul can wear. . . ."

He faded slowly and surely, every hour of pain taking some life out of his soul. He turned to friends for counsel, writing letters full of emotion, saying things such as,

The love of her is a religion to me— it wastes and parches me.

He signed a letter to a student, warning, "my word 'affectionately' means only—that I should have loved people, if I were not dead." He felt that Rose's parents were murdering him, day by day.

Meanwhile, Rose was suffering from various, nameless emotional ailments.

The following Christmas of 1867, when a permitted, promised letter from her did not arrive, Ruskin thought of ending his life. How could he have known that Rose was hardly well enough to write? That her mental state had deteriorated to the point that she was insensible and violent, strapped to a bed in a sanitarium?

Rose recovered from this initial bout of madness. But any feelings she might have had for Ruskin were destroyed when her mother showed her true serpent nature—do you recall her nickname? Maria had written to Effie, questioning Ruskin's ability to be a husband. Effie's murderously spiteful response severed Ruskin from his little pet forever, telling of things that could drive a man to humiliation . . . that he was incapable of making a woman happy, that "he is quite unnatural." (Curiously, if Ruskin *had* married Rose and their union had proven fruitful, the original annulment, based on his presumed impotence, would have been declared wrongful—and Effie's children with Millais would have been made illegitimate. Naturally, Effie was fully aware of this when she wrote to Maria La Touche.)

In the meantime, Ruskin entombed all of Rose's letters in a rosewood box—all but an unbearably beautiful one about the stars and the binding-up of broken hearts. In it, she had written about missing her "Saint C.," and described looking at a star ouside her bedroom window, which made her reflect on man's belief in God:

". . . and then I was thinking of you, it made me think of the guide of the wise men. . . . She [the star] looked down so brightly over the gaslights as if it was intended we should see how much purer and brighter though at such a distance is the Heavenly light if we would only look for it, than our rows of yellow gaslights that we think so much of. Yes, we have a strange Peace on earth, because earth or its inhabitants do not all of them like the Peace that our Prince can give, do not all want it, do not all believe in it."

10

The letter was stamped with her seal in red wax, *Je Reviendrai:* "I will return." Ruskin carried it with him everywhere in a silk pouch between two sheets of gold. Gold, like the tiny plait of Rose's hair, which framed the blue enamel locket he always wore close to his breast. He continued to nourish tender hopes during the next year.

Then, four days after Rose's twenty-first birthday, in 1869, he chanced upon her in the Royal Academy. Rose refused to speak to him. Mutely, he offered her back the precious star letter, unfurling it from the silk pouch. She turned away without a word, leaving the object in his hand.

But their relationship, such as it was, continued to provide both hope and pain for

Ruskin. Ruskin would never forget the summer day in 1872 when he'd been making studies in Venice at the Scuola di San Giorgio degli Schiavoni and had received a letter from Rose calling him to her bedside. He went immediately. There had been a deluded reconciliation as she fell from fever to madness. He made a picture of an olive tree for her. Yet inflammation filled her brain.

The next two months included many long afternoons for Ruskin, spent watching her suffer. Her parents decided he shouldn't visit anymore during this time, so Ruskin and Rose were reduced once again to writing back and forth, Rose both raising and lowering his hopes. Then she wrote a final letter, ending their correspondence. Through a friend, Ruskin asked for

the olive branch drawing
back. He said he wanted to
give her a sketch of hem-
lock instead.

Alas, it wasn't over yet. When Rose
fell ill again, in the fall of 1874, her parents
called Ruskin. His last look at her, writhing in
pain, came in February 1875. She'd lain her
head in his arms as he knelt by her bed.
Afterward, he had slipped out into the dark-
ness, clutching a sketch of her white face against
her pillow. She languished until death, in May of
that year. Ruskin wrote, "I can only get through
my day by fiercely thinking of it, and of nothing
else. . . . The worst of it is that I don't see the
things in front of me well, the blue being taken
out of the sky and the red out of the roses."

2. VENICE, 1876

In 1876, after losing Rose—and when he suffered his first bout of serious instability himself, wandering the streets of Verona in a dressing gown—Ruskin arrived in Venice. To his horror, he found his sorrows augmented. For his delicious Venice had been sadly ravaged and dishonored.

The city had grown old and was falling into greater disrepair each passing day. When restoration did take place, it was crudely oblivious to the history of the architecture. Everywhere Ruskin saw a helpless disintegration that mirrored his own.

Grief had numbed his senses, turning his memories barbed as a wasp's stinger. He wrote to his friend Charles Eliot Norton, "Time was, every hour in Venice was joy to me. Now, I work as I should on a portrait of my mother, dead." In yet another letter, he said, "I live, therefore, simply in continual rage and sorrow."

Ruskin couldn't do anything productive. Instead of delectable prose, he wrote irascible scrags and slivers. Finally, the ink petrified

on his pen, so he took to walking around the city. This didn't save him from feeling desperate: *Stones of Venice* seemed to beguile and

sneer at him from every bookshop window. "I am like a wrecked sailor, picking up the pieces of his ship on the beach," Ruskin wrote.

Ruskin had brought his pain to Venice, and was unable to transfer the colors of his feelings—an intense palette of fear and sorrow—to paper.

Instead, they stained Ruskin's sight. For him, as for any sad lover, the poet Pietro Bembo's roseate palazzo was not, after all, rosy but rinsed in blood. His sadness was like the poor lovelorn nightingale of the fairy tale who impaled himself on a rosebush and dyed the white flowers with his dark blood. Ruskin thought of Bembo pacing the marble floors of his red-rimmed palazzo maddened with love.

If you, reader, have chanced to look at that palazzo, you, too, will remember love. You will remember your lover. You will remember your loss. You will remember the moments when you didn't remember, and you will miss them.

One afternoon during the vaporous winter settling into Venice, Ruskin paused on the Bridge of Sighs, and passed his hand over his wet face. He tried to remember the last time his skin had been as tenderly touched by another's hand, but only the image of Rose on her deathbed appeared in his mind. Between his fingers, he crushed the rose petals that had mysteriously appeared in his pocket and yearned to put his grief to rest.

Under dark, wind-plagued skies he heard the writhing of the slim gondolas straining against the striped paline. He heard the papery sounds of brown crabs clamoring up the stained walls. Bells sobbed in ruined towers. These noises knocked at Ruskin's heart.

Let me out, urged Love, or let me in.

3. Carpaccio's Fairy Tales

Ruskin couldn't bring himself to leave Venice, but he needed some relief from his sorrow. He found it in the fairy-tale paintings of the Venetian artist Vittore Carpaccio.

It wasn't just the beauty of Carpaccio's work that entranced him. He also saw Venice through new eyes—you see, Carpaccio painted astonishing pictures of dragons and knights, of maidens and angels, of oriental potentates and parrots, of saints and barbarians, of journeys and dreams. Although his tales are often set in legendary and far-off lands, the paintings are really portraits of the gorgeous, exotic Venice of the early Renaissance, a town of Turkish traders and Gothic palazzi, of turbans and silken brocades, of silver scimitars and gilded swords. Carpaccio's balconies are overhung with Persian carpets. The ripe buttocks of his gondoliers jut jauntily from kaleidoscopic pantaloons. His jeweled towers and his well-kept campi are the epitome of La Serenissima's serenity.

If you long to imagine Venice in her glory days, fix your gaze on one of the paintings of Carpaccio. His work makes the buildings confess how they are made: gates that look about to swing open, panels inlaid with glowing marble—each painting a sort of blueprint to the architect's secrets.

There was more. Ruskin, whose own faith had been beaten to the transparency of gold leaf, rejoiced in Carpaccio's religious work. Not for Carpaccio the craven saints ducking their heads and twisting their wrists in self-deprecating discomfort. Carpaccio's martyrs and heroes stand naturally, and they look at you with clear eyes.

Ruskin embraced Carpaccio's virgins and princesses, as fair and severe as Rose La Touche. This was a world in which Ruskin could live, in which he could flourish, in which he imagined Rose might reside.

Through these paintings, Ruskin found an intimacy with his Rose. In particular, in the nine-canvas story of Princess Ursula, the legendary evangelizing virgin who became Saint Ursula.[1]

Day after day, Ruskin returned to the Accademia to be enfolded in Ursula's story. He brought his watercolors and made studies of the painting. For weeks, he sat copying her pale sleeping face, as she reminded him of Rose. Not surprisingly, this comforted him.

Saint Ursula slept never-endingly but was alive under Ruskin's paintbrush.

[1] See pages 56–66, "The Carpaccio Gallery," for full reproductions of these paintings.

Ruskin described Ursula's face to his cousin Joan Severn:

There she lies, so real,
that when the room's quiet...
I get afraid of waking her!

And as he worked, trying to re-create the art and cunning of Carpaccio's brush strokes, Ruskin recounted the astonishing tale of Saint Ursula again and again, as if he were telling it to Rose herself. As you will see, it was eerily like Ruskin's own love story.

The first painting depicts two different scenes. In the first, English ambassadors arrive at the colonnaded court of Brittany with a proposal from the King of England, asking that

 his son, Conon, marry Princess Ursula, daughter of the King of Brittany.

But, as Rose would have known, England was a pagan country, while Brittany was Christian. And, like she and Ruskin, Conon and Ursula couldn't marry because of this. Or could they?

In the second scene, Ursula's father speaks to her about the arrangement. She agrees to marry if Conon becomes a Christian, changes his name from the brutish Conon to a spiritual Etherius, and waits three years for the marriage. (Coincidentally, the same length of time Rose had requested.) The couple will also make a pilgrimage to Rome with eleven thousand virgins.

In another of the paintings, ambassadors of Brittany deliver Ursula's letter to the English king, who is attended by an elegantly dressed monkey. (This is Carpaccio's way of showing how ridiculous it is to be a pagan king.) The conditions are accepted and the scene changes to that of Conon, or Etherius, as we must call him now, taking leave of his father and of heathen England. On the sail of his ship, upside down,

droops a shadow of the ill-omened word *malo,* which means "bad fortune."

Ruskin studied the image of Etherius meeting Ursula for the first time, she so pale and serious, as Rose might have been in marriage. The betrothed pair bids farewell to the king and queen, as the Queen Mother wipes away a tear. And, finally, tiny in the background, eleven thousand virgins file onto the ship.

You might notice, as Ruskin did, a scorpion on the flagpole in the center of the painting, a symbol of unsuc-cessful love, evil thoughts, violence, injustice, hidden crimes, and disastrous journeys. . . .

Ursula may have chosen to ignore the scorpion, but that night she dreams of an archangel who predicts a terrible death should she proceed. In the painting, the innocent princess lies asleep, her cheek on her hand. On her windowsill, in a pair of terra-cotta pots, are two symbolic plants. On the left is vervain, sacred to faithful betrothed lovers. On the right is dianthus, which cries in the ardent language of flowers, "I love you."

Despite the dream, Ursula arrives in Rome, where she and Etherius receive the pope's blessing. The pope himself, fired with Ursula's faith, joins the pilgrims on their journey home. His prelates, a sea of tall white hats, look over Ursula's head in Carpaccio's picture.

The pilgrims stop in Cologne, a town under siege from the savage Huns. I suggest you don't look too closely at this next scene, reader. It is terrible. The Hun prince wanted to marry Ursula, and when she refused, he began a massacre that would kill everyone in her party.

In the painting are the virgins and the pope, in their final bloody moments; Etherius is being killed by a dagger, and Ursula kneels as a Hun soldier prepares to shoot an arrow through her heart.

In the final canvas, a radiant Ursula is glo-
riously ascended into Heaven, accompanied by
six athletic putti, the pope, and all the virgins.
Princess Ursula is now Saint Ursula.

In Ruskin's mind, Rose had also become a
saint. He could feel her presence there with him.

4. THE CHRISTMAS STORY

The romance of Venice was becoming less of a torment for Ruskin as he lost himself within the canvases of Carpaccio. For the first time since Rose's death, he felt as if there might be a future for him. He needed but one more thing from Rose before he—before his broken heart—could let go for good. He begged Rose for a sign.

On Christmas Eve, he received such a thing. It was to be only the first of many, a series of remembrances from Rose that for Ruskin would culminate in his rediscovery of Venice as a place of beauty, and of the heart as an organ capable of life and love. But I fear I'm getting ahead of myself here. To December 24, 1876.

Rain had fallen that morning, filling the canals. The gondoliers rowed by in quiet reverence, preparing for a day of movement and holiday excitement. Not one to dally, Ruskin set out early to sketch *The Drunkenness of Noah* in front of Ducal Palace, then was drawn to Carpaccio.

He marveled again at the similarities between his Rose and Carpaccio's princess. Their eyes, their hair—even the very way Ursula reclined under her velvety bed sheets, recalled Rose to Ruskin. His paintbrush balanced in his hand as if it had always belonged there. With heat in his cheeks, Ruskin stroked the paper with color—with reds and oranges. He could almost feel the breeze from Ursula's open windows as it wafted through the dianthus and vervain on the sill, could sense the warmth of her skin under her gown. With a tortured sigh, he left Ursula for the moment and reentered the streets that had, predictably, grown crowded with cheerful anticipation.

The Venetians' happiness didn't disturb Ruskin—

on the contrary, his emotions rose ever higher as he returned to his room to find that Carpaccio's flowers had come to life. It was a sign, a lesson, a true reason to rejoice. For a dried sprig of vervain had been sent to him by the botanist at Kew Gardens. A pot of dianthus, too, with a single pink blossom, arrived from a friend, with a note:

From Saint Ursula,
out of her bedroom window,
with love.

Ruskin felt sure that Rose—Saint Rose—was sending him a message. He was in ecstasy.

Were the signs really there? Was Ruskin ready to believe? He was, after all, a storyteller

and a poet. Could he believe

in spirits when he didn't even

believe in a God?

Yet something was happening

to him—something he could not

explain, even as he tried. He rose early on

Christmas Day, still believing. After a morning

of joyous, easy writing, he set out on foot,

vividly alive and attuned to all that Venice

offered. Tableaux of her lovers and their ghosts

cheered him from their picturesque locales. He

imagined lovers on the bridges, in gondolas,

leaning out windows, and whispering in dim

cafés, reminding him of what he'd lost and also

of what he'd once had. And perhaps, hoped

Ruskin, having lost everything, he might find

something to nourish his heart again.

Rose continued to help. She returned Ruskin to the nursery of his mind for days of calming restoration. On Christmas Day, a murex shell was given to him as a small gift. Once part of the sea, the shell—a miracle of nature in itself—was exactly like the one in Carpaccio's painting *Saint George and the Dragon,* and, significantly, like "the black and white one I was painting when the Master's [Mr. La Touche] refusal came to let me see Rosie in London," explained Ruskin. "This was Saint Ursula's order to forgive this Master."

In a dreamlike state, Ruskin wandered around the city, visiting friends. In the early afternoon, he brought good wishes to his gondolier, whose daughter was so breathtakingly beautiful that Ruskin compared her to a Madonna.

Once again the magic of Venice, the maze of its streets and canals, caught Ruskin unawares and brought him a joyful bolt of recognition. *This* was the Venice he'd wanted to see again, the Venice that would make him whole again. He was so caught up in the beauty of it, in his sheer relief at recognizing it again—and distracted, too, by his thoughts of the lovely Madonna-like creature he'd just met—that he didn't pay attention to where he was going and found himself at the Scuola di San Giorgio degli Schiavoni. "Oh—I said to myself, Little Bear means me to finish *here*."

Inside the scuola, it was cozy, enchanting. Redemption was to be found under the low beams painted in naïve *trompes l'oeil*. Ruskin took inventory of the treasures—the Carpaccios of Saint George. The effect was instant; words started to fill him like honey. These pictures, he wrote, glow like "embers on some peaceful hearth, cast up into the room where one sits waiting for dear friends, in twilight... or like a tapestry for a Christmas night in a home a thousand years old...."

He recalled Christmases past, with Rose curled at his feet listening to his stories, safe but excited in the net of his words, captured and led where his imagination wanted her to go. Saint George was always her favorite, and she would look to him adoringly as he shared his knowledge with her. These were fairy tales, to be sure, made up to transport their viewers to another time and place. And it was Carpaccio's Saint George, Carpaccio's dragon, and Carpaccio's little princess that Ruskin always saw in his mind when he told the tale to Rose....

In the story of Saint George, as Ruskin and Carpaccio both told it, a malicious and gluttonous dragon infested the town of Selene in North Africa, devouring two children each

week. Finally, only the pale, fair Princess of Selene was left for him to eat. Just as he was about to devour her, the heroic Saint George arrived to kill the dragon.

It was the sort of moment Ruskin might have wished for himself and Rose.

Moving from painting to painting with mounting excitement, Ruskin noticed for the first time that the red bird in the Baptism painting was a Porphyrio, the bird of eternal rebirth, and that it was feasting on a piece of vervain plant. "That's enough, Little Bear, for today—I can't take any more," he said. Ruskin knelt under the Saint Jerome to give his thanks "and was just going out of the door when I saw the bronze

crucifix in front of it. . . . So I kissed the feet—
which I had never yet done in any chapel. . . ."

The crucifix that had meant nothing to
Ruskin for all this time—since he'd heard the
sermon in Turin in 1858 that made him doubt
everything that he'd ever believed, and certainly
organized religion—had drawn him in, and
he, knowing that it was what Rose wanted,
embraced what it stood for.

The afternoon was waning as Ruskin
called for a gondolier to take him home. The
combination of the Madonna, the Porphyrio,
the blessing at the crucifix: It had been alto-
gether an overwhelming day. Then his gondolier
appeared, "a horrid monster with inflamed
eyes, red as coals." Ruskin first turned him away
with disgust, then wondered if Rose had meant

for his kindness to be tested. He followed the man to a boat with filthy cushions, but when the man again fixed his red, red eyes on him, Ruskin stepped away.

Arriving home for his Christmas dinner, Ruskin mused that the Madonna *and* Lucifer really had appeared to him. Thinking of Christ, and the dinner at Cana when water is turned into wine, Ruskin drank only water at his Christmas dinner.

Alas, his water tasted only of water, not wine, and in the morning, Ruskin began to even doubt the gifts—the signs—the *lesson*—he had received. But then he returned to the Accademia to work on his study of the sleeping Saint Ursula, troubled by her brow as he'd drawn it. He stood with the blue locket in his hand. Rose's golden hair in its plaited border might have been spun from Saint Ursula's plaits. Rose and Ursula were entangled in his mind. The portrait wasn't quite right—Ruskin grew distraught, then realized that the devil was trying to distort his talents. He struggled against him and found his way again. Of the moment he wrote,

I was... shewn the full meaning of the end of the Lord's prayer, which I had never in my life understood.

As Rose would have wished—did wish, throughout her short adulthood—Ruskin had found his God.

5. ACQUA ALTA

The week after Christmas, Ruskin worked again in the Accademia Gallery, copying the painting of Saint Ursula. His mood was rising. He felt an *acqua alta,* a high tide, flushing his own arteries, stirring something warm into the old life-fluids of ink and oil. He divided his time between the inky notebook and the oily canvas. He dropped the pen to pick up the

paintbrush then clenched the brush in his teeth to scribble some words. They fell in clean, good formation on the white page. The paint clustered richly and fragrantly on his brush and then sidled off, with glutinous but disciplined luxuriousness, onto his canvas.

He took a long walk, imagining that Rose was watching from Heaven while he wandered the watery streets. Close to his breast, as always, were the blue locket and the silk pouch with its star letter.

He crossed the Piazza San Marco and inhaled with the rapture he always felt at the sight of the Basilica. His eyes lighted on the mother-of-pearl pillars and slid over the opaline corbels. The Basilica was encrusted with mosaics, bronze horses, angels, pomegranates. And inside! A magpie's nest of plundered coral, alabaster, and Byzantine gold!

There was water in the Piazza from the tide. Ruskin watched the surface of the water tighten to a reflective lens, and suddenly there were two Basilicas, one bright, one pale. A

double-headed Campanile seemed nailed into the belly of the earth. Like all Venetian mirrors, this one was speckled: The silver water was dusted with tiny white feathers shed by the pigeons. White feathers, white like the lace on Rose's confirmation dress, the handkerchief she had waved at him from her bedroom window.

Ruskin began walking toward the Rialto. He carried with him still the memory of 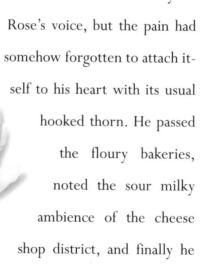 Rose's voice, but the pain had somehow forgotten to attach itself to his heart with its usual hooked thorn. He passed the floury bakeries, noted the sour milky ambience of the cheese shop district, and finally he breathed in the cool salt stench of the fish market.

The day's catch lay scintillating in pink, gray, and black, as it had done for a thousand years. The tourists eyed the fleshy langoustines and silky trout, helplessly envious of the Venetian housewives, able to turn the jeweled fish into dinner instead of mere spectacle. He glanced across the Grand Canal toward the Ca' d'Oro, the golden palace he loved to look at—and to paint.

Ruskin contemplated the difference between observing and creating, watching and writing. He himself could never bear to be a dumb witness to anything beautiful. He mapped his journey in his mind, from the dark haunts of the markets to the shimmering waters of the canals. And he also sketched the map of his heart, the map of burnt-out areas now ready to be irrigated with tears, of floodscapes prepared for sunshine, of intellect welcoming feeling, a map of where life had taken Ruskin, a heart-shaped map, made in Venice.

He walked toward Arsenale, the fortress of Venice, and turned away from the sea. He wanted to look at the row of stone lions just

outside the gates of the naval fortress. Ruskin released a short grunt of a laugh when he saw a cat sitting on the head of the tallest lion, his pearly paws covering its vacant eyes, a tail draped round its undeniably silly jowls. How Rosie would have giggled.

He could almost hear the sound of her hands clapping in joy. Rosie's voice, a ghost of games and stories past, swirled gracefully around him and swallowed him up in vivid memories. Almost expecting the cat to leap from its majestic perch, Ruskin paused in thought. "Paint me a picture of those silly lions in Venice," he imagined her begging him, "please," secure in the knowledge that he would kill and skin them for her just to win that laugh back.

In a sense, he *had* won her back. She had represented innocence and youth to him, when he'd needed this most—and Ruskin had been able to lose himself in her life for a time. Now it was over. *Venice asks too much of us,* he reflected, *by the relentless standard of romance she sets.* It occurred to Ruskin that maybe he had asked too much of Rose. Perhaps he'd expected too much from himself, too. In her own way, she *had* loved him. And brought upon him the love of many others.

The gentle lilt of Rosie's happy laughter filled his soul for a moment, until it drifted away, only to be replaced by the sound of a gondolier singing in the canal.

With a shiver, Ruskin quickly recognized the ballad from Carpaccio's portrait of Saint

Augustine. In the painting, the artist himself had rendered the notes so meticulously that Ruskin could—and had—hummed them aloud. It was a ballad of love and longing, joy and belief, one that had been sung in Venice for centuries.

Ruskin tucked the memory of the moment into his heart, where it would remain, whenever he needed it.

THE ARRIVAL OF THE ENGLISH
AMBASSADORS AT THE COURT
·
OF THE KING OF BRITTANY

THE DISMISSAL OF THE AMBASSADORS

THE RETURN OF THE AMBASSADORS

THE MEETING AND DEPARTURE
OF THE BETROTHED COUPLE

THE DREAM OF SAINT URSULA

THE MEETING OF THE PILGRIMS WITH THE
POPE, UNDER THE WALLS OF ROME

THE ARRIVAL AT COLOGNE

THE MARTYRDOM
OF THE PILGRIMS
AND THE FUNERAL
OF SAINT URSULA

THE APOTHEOSIS OF SAINT URSULA
AND HER ATTENDANTS

Notes to
the Reader

Authors' Notes

You may be doubting how much of this story is true. Using letters, diaries, and Ruskin's autobiography, however, we have tried to present as honest a recounting as possible.

Ruskin certainly became obsessed with Carpaccio's Saint Ursula, in whom he saw such an astonishing resemblance to Rose La Touche. He wrote of this often with passion in his letters. In addition, he himself called the week of receiving signs from Rose his "Christmas Story." Ruskin felt that something wonderful and strange was occurring on those days, beginning the morning of Sunday, December 24, and ending on Tuesday, January 2, 1877, when "my ordinary life began again." He recorded the events in diary-letters to Joan Severn.

As for Rose La Touche and his relationship with her, things are a bit more vague. Soon after the events of this story, Ruskin's friend and one of his executors, Charles Eliot Norton, wrote that Ruskin's heirs should "make a holocaust of his correspondence. I dread the vultures that are already hovering over what they have long marked for their prey." No doubt, he feared the exposure of Ruskin's relationship with Rose.

And so it was that nearly everything to do with her, including all their correspondence (returned by the La Touche family), was likely destroyed by Severn and Norton in June 1900, in a bonfire in Ruskin's little woodland garden, overlooked by a wild rose. In those flames perished what were undoubtedly the most beautiful and tormented letters Ruskin ever wrote.

The story of Rose was not extinguished, however. Fragments of her diaries were discovered by scholar Helen Gill Viljoen, at Brantwood, in 1929. Alas, they soon disappeared. Letters to, from, and about Rose continue to emerge. Her wraith has begun to substantiate.

Death is but a cursory barrier to a love already denied. Ruskin, interested in spiritualism, had Rose conjured up at seances. Her letter-seal really did bear the words *Je Reviendrai:* "I will return."

As for Vittore Carpaccio's paintings, they can still be seen in Venice today. The descriptions of them in this book are mostly adapted from a series of newsletters Ruskin penned, called the *Fors Clavigera,* as well as his book *St. Mark's Rest,* and his diaries and letters.

The Saint Ursula cycle was originally commissioned for her own scuola near the church of San Giovanni e Paolo. When the scuola was suppressed in 1806 by Napoleon, the pictures moved to their current home in the Accademia Gallery. The original paintings of Saint George, Saint Tryphon, and Saint Augustine are still in the Scuola Dalmata dei Santi Giorgio e Trifone (usually known as the Scuola di San Giorgio degli Schiavoni).

Cast of Characters

(in order of appearance)

JOHN RUSKIN (1819–1900) was an English art critic, artist, designer, philosopher, and prolific writer. Best known for *Modern Painters* (1843–1860) and *Stones of Venice* (1851–1853), he tried to change the public's attitude toward art, religion, and economics.

EUPHEMIA GRAY (known as Effie) (1828–1897) was Ruskin's wife from 1848 to 1854. The marriage was annulled on grounds of nonconsummation. The following year she married the painter John Millais.

SIR JOHN EVERETT MILLAIS (1829–1896) was an English painter and member of the Pre-Raphaelite Brotherhood. While painting a portrait of Ruskin, Millais fell in love with Ruskin's wife, Effie, whom he later married.

ROSE LA TOUCHE (1849–1875) was the young Irish woman Ruskin loved. Though he lost her to madness and brain fever (meningitis) at age twenty-seven, Ruskin felt she knew him better than anyone. He wrote, "Rose, in my heart, was with me always, and all I did was for her sake."

MARIA AND JOHN LA TOUCHE, Rose's parents.
John was a stern, religious Irish banker, whose strict
Calvinist beliefs may have contributed to Rose's mental
instability. Maria wrote novels and exchanged letters
on botany and many other subjects with Ruskin, even
after her daughter's death.

CHARLES ELIOT NORTON (1827–1908), an American
writer, critic, and professor, was Ruskin's friend and
admirer. As one of Ruskin's executors, he helped burn
the letters between Ruskin and Rose La Touche.

VITTORE CARPACCIO (c. 1465–c. 1527), now one of
Venice's most famous artists, died in complete obscu-
rity. His work is in most major sites in the city.

JOAN SEVERN (née Agnew) (1846–1924), a distant
cousin of Ruskin's, looked after him in his old age and
inherited his estate. As a Ruskin executor, Joan burned
the correspondence between Ruskin and Rose La Touche.

SAINT URSULA, the legendary evangelizing virgin
princess whose story Carpaccio painted, probably lived
in the fourth century.

Ruskin's Venetian Haunts

THE BASILICA OF SAN MARCO is the great church of Venice. The Venetians stole the body of Saint Mark from Alexandria, Egypt, and brought him to their city in the ninth century. The church was originally built in his honor, and was, for many years, the private chapel of the Doges. Its interior and exterior are richly decorated with treasures from the Crusades. The entire ceiling is encrusted with golden mosaics.

THE BRIDGE OF SIGHS links the Palazzo Ducale to the rooms in the "New Prisons," in which offenders would be questioned. The bridge was so christened by the Romantic writers, who imagined the feelings of prisoners passing over it, catching their last glimpse of the beautiful Venetian lagoon before their incarceration.

THE CA' D'ORO ("Golden House"), an ornate colonnaded palace on the Grand Canal dating to 1440, is considered the finest example of Venetian Gothic architecture. Its name comes from the ultramarine, vermilion, and gold leaf that once decorated its facade. It still looks golden at sunset, particularly in the winter. Ruskin called it "the noblest place on the Grand Canal" and painted it in 1845.

THE CAMPANILE has
served Venice as a bell tower,
lighthouse, and watchtower. The
original building, completed in 1514,
collapsed in 1902 but was rebuilt in perfect
facsimile within a decade.

THE DRUNKENNESS OF NOAH is an early fifteenth-
century sculpture, set on the corner of the Palazzo
Ducale, facing the lagoon and just in front of the
Bridge of Sighs. It symbolizes the frailty of man.

THE GALLERIE DELL'ACCADEMIA, in the Dorsoduro
quarter of Venice, houses the largest collection of
Venetian art from the fourteenth to the eighteenth
centuries. The Accademia has been in its present
premises, in three former religious buildings on the
banks of the Grand Canal, since 1807. It contains
works from the Academy of Fine Arts, established in
1750, and also art removed from monasteries,
convents, and churches by order of Napoleon.
Carpaccio's Saint Ursula cycle is there, taken from its
original chapel near San Giovanni e Paolo, as are a
series of exquisite Madonnas by Giovanni Bellini.

THE GRAND CANAL has been called the most beautiful street in the world. Known as the "Canalazzo" by the Venetians, it winds for two miles through the heart of Venice, fronted on both sides by exquisite Byzantine, Gothic, and Renaissance palaces, churches, and gardens.

THE PALAZZO BEMBO is said to be the birthplace of the poet Pietro Bembo. The rose-pink walls of this fifteenth-century Gothic palace, on the Rio di San Salvatore, can be easily viewed from the Rialto Bridge.

THE PALAZZO DUCALE or Doge's Palace was the seat of Venetian government from the earliest days of the Republic in the ninth century until its fall in 1797. It was the official home of the Doge, the head of the Venetian state. It also served as the Palace of Justice,

and was the prison where Casanova was incarcerated in the eighteenth century. During his visit to Venice in 1876–1877, Ruskin was reading Casanova's account of his escape from the dreaded "Leads," the lead-roofed prisons about the palace. This glorious Gothic palace is sumptuously decorated inside with frescoes and paintings, including Carpaccio's famous *Winged Lion of Venice*.

THE PIAZZA SAN MARCO is the great square at the heart of Venice. At its edges are the Basilica, the Palazzo Ducale, the Campanile, and the Piazzetta. Napoleon called the superbly elegant Piazza, which he remodeled, "the drawing room of Europe."

THE ROYAL ACADEMY OF ARTS is an early eighteenth-century mansion in London's West End, home to the Royal Academy founded in 1768, and an art school. Many of Britain's finest artists have been "Academicians."

THE SCUOLA DI SAN GIORGIO DEGLI SCHIAVONI was the chapel of the large Dalmatian (Schiavoni) community in northeast Venice, situated in Castello. The scuola—a religious and cultural establishment— commissioned Vittore Carpaccio to paint stories of its patron saints, George, Tryphon, and Jerome. The work was done between 1502 and 1507.

TIME LINE OF RUSKIN'S LIFE

February 18, 1819 Ruskin is born in London to
wealthy sherry importer John James Ruskin and
Margaret Cox.

1835 Ruskin tours France, Switzerland, and Italy.

1837 Ruskin enters Oxford University.

1840 Ruskin spends the winter in Italy.

1843–1860 Ruskin works on and publishes *Modern
Painters* (five volumes).

1845 Ruskin's first visit to Venice.

1848 Ruskin marries Effie Gray.

1849 Ruskin again visits Venice, this time with
his new bride, Effie. He works on *Stones of Venice*,
a guide to the architecture of Venice. *The Seven Lamps
of Architecture* is published.

1851–1853 *Stones of Venice* (three volumes) is published.

July 1854 Ruskin's marriage to Effie is annulled.

July 1855 Effie marries John Millais.

1858 Ruskin abandons his Protestant faith after a
sermon in Turin. Rose La Touche enters his life.

1862 Periodic separations from Rose begin when her
parents become uneasy about the relationship. Ruskin
publishes *Unto This Last*.

1864 Ruskin's father dies.

1865 *Sesame and Lilies* is published.

1867 Rose's first bout of madness. Ruskin publishes *Time and Tide.*

1869–1879 Ruskin becomes Slade Professor of Fine Art at Oxford.

1871 Ruskin starts a magazine, *Fors Clavigera,* covering art, politics, economics, and personal matters.

May 26, 1875 Rose dies of "brain fever"—probably some form of meningitis. Ruskin recovers all his letters to and from her.

1876 The last but one of Ruskin's journeys to Venice.

1877 Ruskin returns to England. He attacks the artist James McNeill Whistler in *Fors.* Ruskin loses the libel case subsequently brought against him by Whistler. He is too ill to attend the trial.

1878 Ruskin's first attack of madness.

1879 Ruskin resigns from the Slade professorship.

1886 Ruskin's autobiography, *Praeterita,* is published.

January 20, 1900 Ruskin dies at his home at Brantwood. A plaque is erected in his memory in Venice.

June 1900 Joan Severn and Charles Eliot Norton burn all the Rose La Touche letters.

BIBLIOGRAPHY

Benson, Arthur. *Ruskin: A Study in Personality*. London: Smith,
    Elder, & Co., 1911.

Burd, Van Akin, ed. *John Ruskin and Rose La Touche: Her Unpublished
    Diaries of 1861 and 1867*. Oxford: Clarendon Press, 1979.

————, ed. *The Winnington Letters: John Ruskin's Correspondence with
    Margaret Alexis Bell and the Children at Winnington Hall*. Cambridge,
    Massachusetts: Belknap/Harvard University Press, 1969.

————. *Christmas Story: John Ruskin's Venetian Letters of 1876–1877*.
    Newark: University of Delaware Press, 1990.

Clark, Sir Kenneth. *Ruskin and His Circle*. London:
    The Arts Council, 1964.

Clegg, Jeanne. *Ruskin and Venice*. London: Junction Books, 1981.

Dearden, James. *Ruskin, Bembridge and Brantwood*. Keele University
    Press, Ryburn Publishing, 1994.

Evans, Joan. *John Ruskin*. London: Jonathan Cape, 1954.

Fleming, John, Hugh Honour, and Nikolaus Pevsner.
    A Dictionary of Architecture. Harmondsworth, England:
    Penguin Books Ltd., 1966.

Harris, Cyril M., ed. *Illustrated Dictionary of Historic Architecture*.
    New York: Dover Publications, Inc., 1977.

Hewison, Robert. *John Ruskin: The Argument of the Eye*. London:
    Thames & Hudson, 1976.

————. *Ruskin and Venice*. London: Thames & Hudson, 1978.

Molmenti, Pompeo, and Gustav Ludwig. *The Life and Works of
    Vittorio Carpaccio*, trans. Robert H. Hobart Cust. London:
    John Murray, 1907.

Moschini, Vittorio. *Carpaccio: La Leggenda di Sant'Orsola*. Milano:
    Edizioni D'Arte Amilcare Pizzi, 1949.

Orr, Chris. *Chris Orr's John Ruskin*, with notes and an essay by
    Robert Hewison. London: Signford, 1976.

Pignatti, Terisio. *Carpaccio,* trans. James Emmons. Milan, Italy:
    Skira, 1958.

Ruskin, John. *Correspondence of John Ruskin to Charles Eliot Norton*, ed. John Lewis Bradley and Ian Ousby. Cambridge: Cambridge University Press, 1987.

——. *The Diaries of John Ruskin*, ed. Joan Evans and John Whitehouse, 3 vols. Oxford: Clarendon Press, 1956–1959.

——. *The Eagle's Nest* (lecture), from *Collected Works*. New York: J. W. Lovell & Co., 1886.

——. *Fors Clavigera*. Self-published newsletter, 1871–1878.

——. *Guide to the Principal Pictures in the Academy of Fine Arts at Venice*. Venice: 1877.

——. *The Gulf of Years: Letters from John Ruskin to Kathleen Olander*, commentary by Kathleen Prynne, ed. with a Preface by Rayner Unwin. London: Allen & Unwin Ltd., 1953.

——. *Letters of John Ruskin to Charles Eliot Norton*, 2 vols. Boston: Houghton, Mifflin and Company, 1904.

——. *Letters of John Ruskin to Lord and Lady Mount-Temple*, ed. John Lewis Bradley. Columbus, Ohio: Ohio State University Press, 1964.

——. *Praeterita: Outlines of Scenes and Thoughts Perhaps Worthy of Memory in My Past Life*, Introduction by Kenneth Clark. London: Rupert Hart-Davis, 1949.

——. *Stones of Venice*, 3 vols. London: George Allen, 1905.

——. *St. Mark's Rest: The History of Venice*. London: George Allen, 1894.

Sgarbi, Vittorio. *Carpaccio*. New York: Abbeville Press, 1995.

Vasari, Giorgio. *Lives of the Painters, Sculptors, and Architects,* trans. Gaston de Vere, 2 vols. London: Everyman's Library, 1996.

Williams-Ellis, Amabel. *The Tragedy of John Ruskin*. London: Jonathan Cape, 1928.

Young, Margaret Ferrier, ed. *The Letters of a Noble Woman (Mrs. La Touche of Harristown)*. London: George Allen & Sons, 1908.

Zorzi, Ludovico. *Carpaccio e la rappresentazione di Sant'Orsola*. Torino: Giulio Einaudi Editore, .1988.

Zucconi, Guido. *Venice: An Architectural Guide,* trans. Anthony Shugaar. Venice: Arsenale Editrice, 1993.

Acknowledgments
and Permissions

With thanks to James Dearden, Howard Hull, Professore
Giandomenico Romanelli (Direttore, Civici Musei
Veneziani D'Arte e di Storia), Commissario Tullio Vallery
(Guardian Grande della Scuola Dalmata dei Santi Giorgio
e Trifone), Dottoressa Giovanna Nepie Sciré (Soprinten-
dente, Ministero per i Beni Culturali e Ambientali di
Venezia), Signorina Lombardo (Resp. Ufficio Stampa
Assessorato Alla Cultura). Thanks also to Van Akin Burd,
whose wonderful book *Christmas Story: John Ruskin's Venetian
Letters of 1876–1877*, has been an invaluable source on this
time in Ruskin's life.

Carpaccio details, pages 41, 55, courtesy of the Scuola
    Dalmata dei Santi Giorgio e Trifone, Venice.
Carpaccio details, pages 20 (middle and right), 23, 24,
    27, 28, 31, 56–66, courtesy of the Accademia Gallery,
    Venice.
Carpaccio detail, page 20 (left), courtesy of Erich
    Lessing/Art Resource, NY.
Self-portrait of John Ruskin, page 32, courtesy of
    The Pierpont Morgan Library/Art Resource, NY.
Portrait of Rose La Touche by John Ruskin, page 32,
    courtesy of The Ruskin Foundation (Ruskin Library,
    University of Lancaster).